AMAZING SCIENCE
THE SOLAR SYSTEM

Written by
Rebecca Phillips-Bartlett

Genius Kid

North Star
KIDS

The Solar System © 2024 BookLife Publishing
This edition is published by arrangement with BookLife Publishing

sales@northstareditions.com | 888-417-0195

Library of Congress Control Number:
2024952962

ISBN
978-1-952455-27-8 (library bound)
978-1-952455-83-4 (paperback)
978-1-952455-65-0 (epub)
978-1-952455-47-6 (hosted ebook)

Printed in the United States of America
Mankato, MN
092025

Written by:
Rebecca Phillips-Bartlett

Edited by:
Elise Carraway

Designed by:
Ker Ker Lee

All facts, statistics, web addresses and URLs in this book were verified as valid and accurate at time of writing. No responsibility for any changes to external websites or references can be accepted by either the author or publisher.

Photo Credits – Images are courtesy of Shutterstock.com. With thanks to Getty Images, Thinkstock Photo and iStockphoto.

Cover – Anan Kaewkhammul, Andrey_Kuzmin, Eric Isselee, NASA / JPL / Space Science Institute, oksana2010, red-feniks, Tony Campbell, Vac1. 2–3 – ooodles. 4–5 – chrisbrignell, Eric Isselee, Jane Koshchina. 6–7 – jeep2499, Eric Isselee, Felineusl. 8–9 – KDdesign_photo_video, RJ22, Ukki Studio. 10–11 – Eric Isselee, Nynke van Holten, allme, Kirill Vorobyev. 12–13 – Nynke van Holten, Nejron Photo, Eric Isselee, 5 second Studio, Nynke van Holten, FCG, Evgeniia Trushkova, Irina Gutyryak. 14–15 – ANURAK PONGPATIMET, Dora Zett. 16–17 – Cat Box, Eric Isselee. 18–19 – Nataliia Maksymenko, Kuttelvaserova Stuchelova, Ermolaev Alexander. 20–21 – QBR, Max Acronym, BetterTomorrow, Vikafoto33. 22–23 – Max kegfirem, Andrey_Kuzmin, Eric Isselee, Vaclav Matous, Nynke van Holten.

CONTENTS

Words that look like this can be found in the glossary on page 24.

THE SOLAR SYSTEM

Have you ever looked up at the sky and wondered what is out there?

We live on a planet in a huge <u>universe</u>. Within this universe, we are part of the solar system.

The solar system is a collection of planets and other space objects. They move around a star called the sun.

DID YOU KNOW?

People used to think Earth was the center of the universe.

Now we know that isn't true at all.

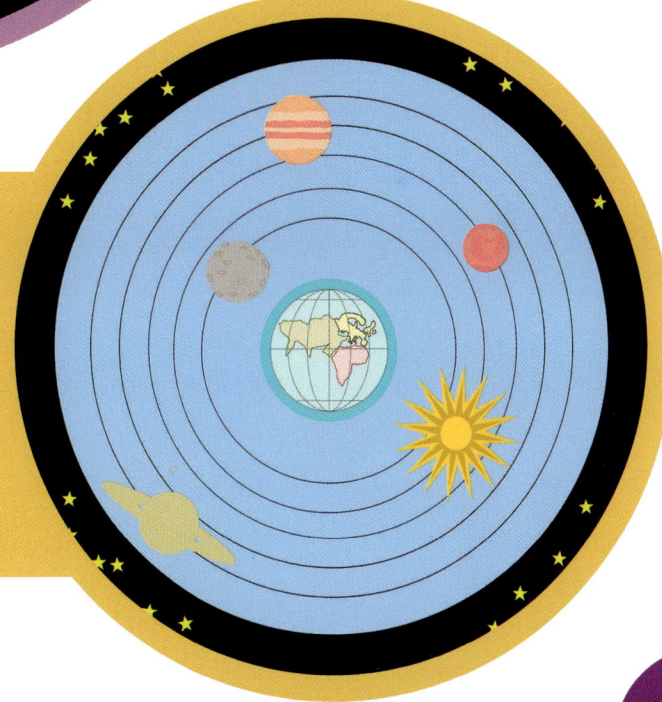

KEY WORDS

Here are some key words about space every genius kid should learn.

ORBIT

An orbit is when an object travels in a circle around another object.

YEAR

A year is the amount of time it takes a planet to orbit its star. It takes Earth about 365 days to orbit the sun.

DAY

Each planet spins around an imaginary line called an axis. The time it takes a planet to spin around its axis once makes up one day.

Axis

GRAVITY

Gravity is a <u>force</u> that pulls objects toward one another.

THE SUN

The sun is the star at the center of our solar system.

The sun is the largest object in our solar system. Its gravity is strong enough to hold the entire solar system together.

DID YOU KNOW?
The sun is the only star in our solar system.

A star is a hot ball of burning gas. The sun makes lots of heat and light. We can feel the sun's light and heat on Earth. People need this heat and light to live.

THE PLANETS

Our solar system contains eight planets.

To be a planet, an object in space must:

- Orbit a star
- Be round like a ball
- Be big enough that its gravity has cleared all other objects of similar size from its <u>orbital path</u>

The eight planets are called:

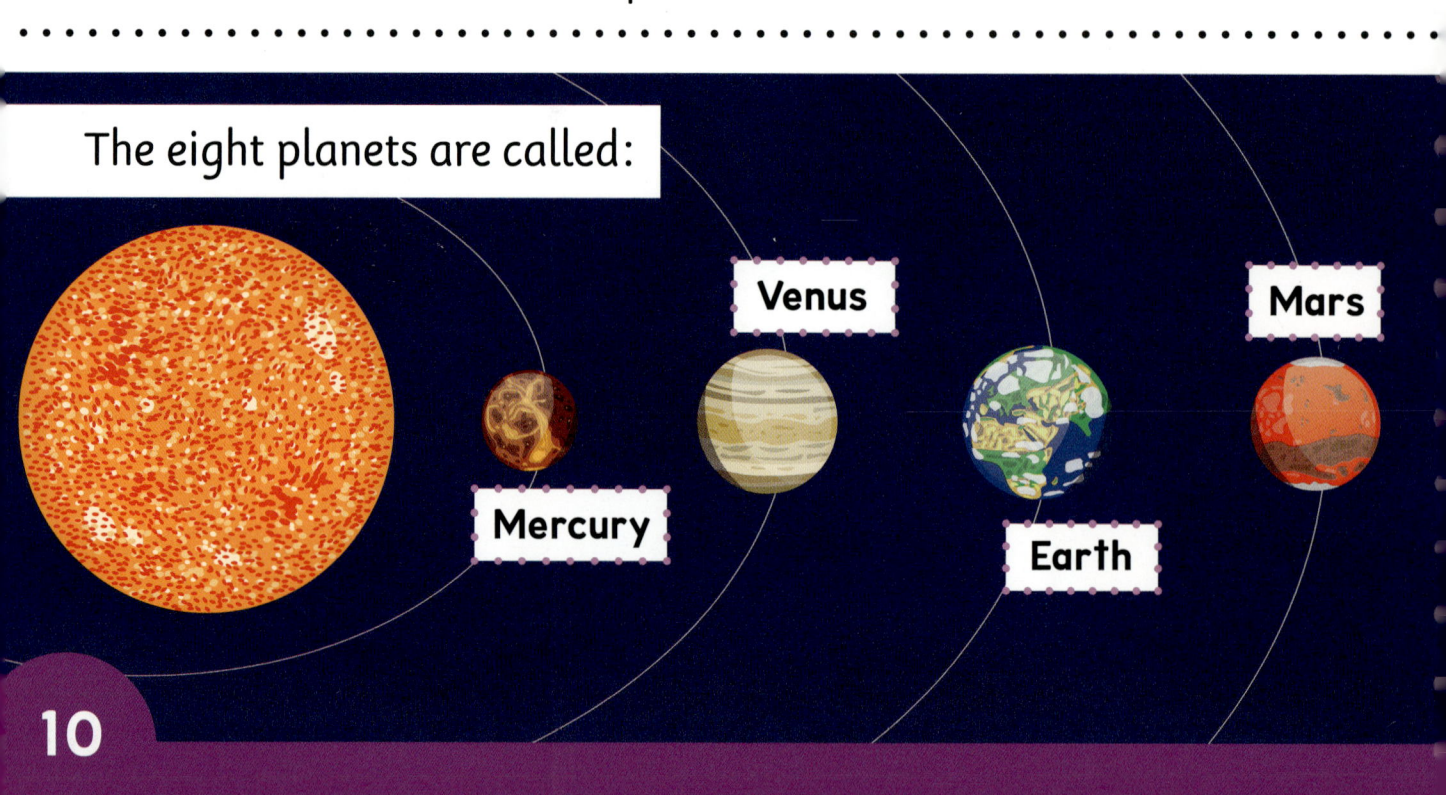

Mercury

Venus

Earth

Mars

Do you want to remember the order of the planets? This <u>mnemonic device</u> might help!

My **V**ery **E**xcellent **M**other **J**ust **S**erved **U**s **N**oodles.

Jupiter

Saturn

Uranus

Neptune

SATELLITES

A satellite is any object that orbits a planet or a star. Earth is a satellite. It orbits the sun.

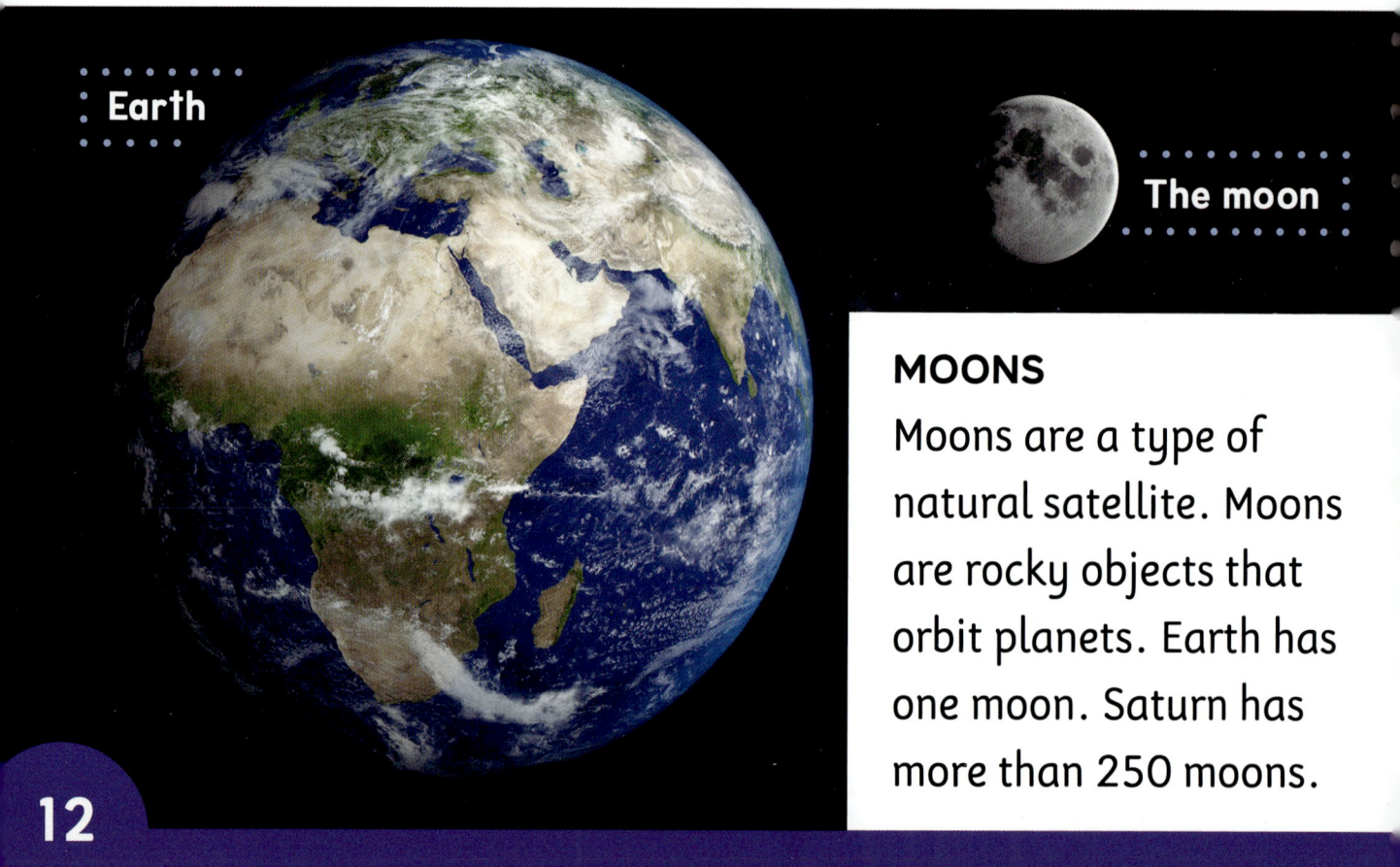

Earth

The moon

MOONS

Moons are a type of natural satellite. Moons are rocky objects that orbit planets. Earth has one moon. Saturn has more than 250 moons.

The International
Space Station

HUMAN-MADE SATELLITES

Some satellites have been made by
people. These satellites help us learn
more about Earth and space. Some
scientists live inside the International
Space Station. This satellite orbits
Earth.

Turn to page 16
to learn more
about human-made
satellites.

OTHER SPACE OBJECTS

DWARF PLANETS

Dwarf planets do not meet all the rules to be a planet. They are too small.

THE ASTEROID BELT

Asteroids are lumps of rock and metal in space. The asteroid belt is an area where many asteroids orbit the sun.

COMETS

Comets are made of rock, dust, and ice. In the sky, comets have bright, glowing tails.

The asteroid belt is between Mars and Jupiter.

THE KUIPER BELT

The Kuiper Belt is a ring of icy space objects. It includes comets and icy dwarf planets. It is just outside Neptune's orbit.

A TIMELINE OF SPACE TRAVEL

1957
Humans <u>launched</u> the first satellite, *Sputnik 1*, in October. In November, *Sputnik 2* carried a dog into orbit.

1969
Neil Armstrong and Buzz Aldrin became the first people to walk on the moon.

1961
Yuri Gagarin became the first person in space and the first person to orbit Earth.

16

1990

The Hubble Space Telescope was sent into orbit. It orbits Earth. It takes photographs and collects information.

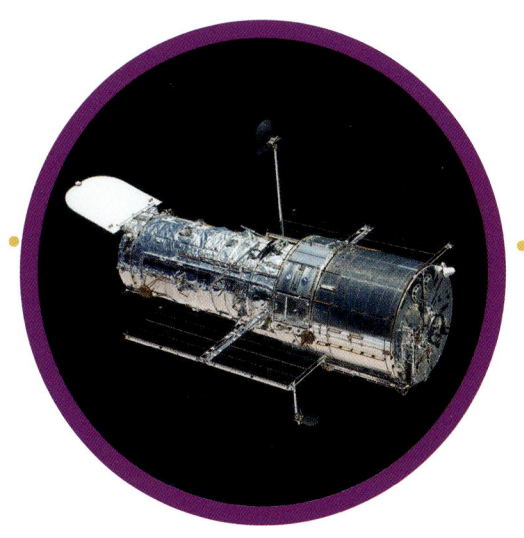

1997

The first Mars rover landed on Mars. Mars rovers are robots. They drive around the planet. Scientists use them to collect data.

1998

The International Space Station was launched. It has been home to more than 250 astronauts.

BEYOND THE SOLAR SYSTEM

Our solar system is a small part of a huge universe. So, what lies beyond the solar system?

The solar system is thought to be surrounded by the Oort Cloud. This is a giant bubble of icy objects.

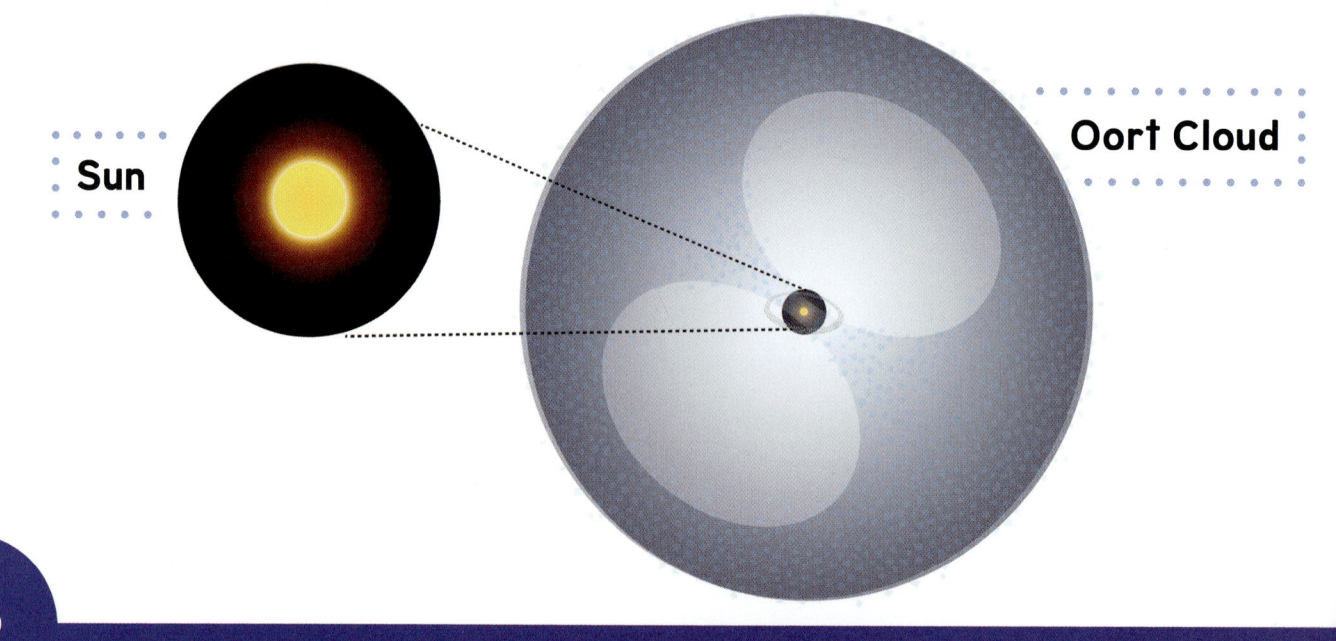

Sun

Oort Cloud

Zoom out farther. You will discover galaxies. A galaxy is a huge collection of gas, dust, and stars. There are many galaxies. Our solar system is in a galaxy called the Milky Way.

DID YOU KNOW?
Sometimes it's possible to see parts of the Milky Way from Earth.

BELIEVE IT OR NOT!

Have you ever seen a shooting star? It wasn't a star at all! Shooting stars are pieces of space rock that have flown into Earth's <u>atmosphere</u>. When rocks enter Earth's atmosphere, they begin to burn.

Until 2006, the dwarf planet Pluto was thought to be a planet.

Except Earth, the planets in the solar system are named after Roman or Greek gods.

Neptune

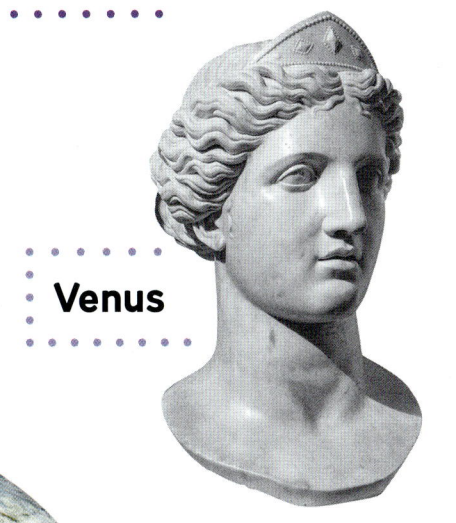

Venus

Mars

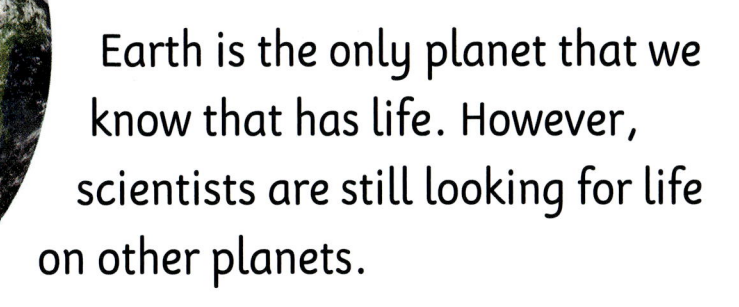

Earth is the only planet that we know that has life. However, scientists are still looking for life on other planets.

ARE YOU A GENIUS KID?

You are now full of out-of-this-world solar system facts to impress your friends and family with. But first, it is time to test your knowledge! Are you truly a genius kid?

Check back through the book if you are not sure.

1. How many planets are in the solar system?

2. Who was the first person to go into space?

3. What is the Oort Cloud?

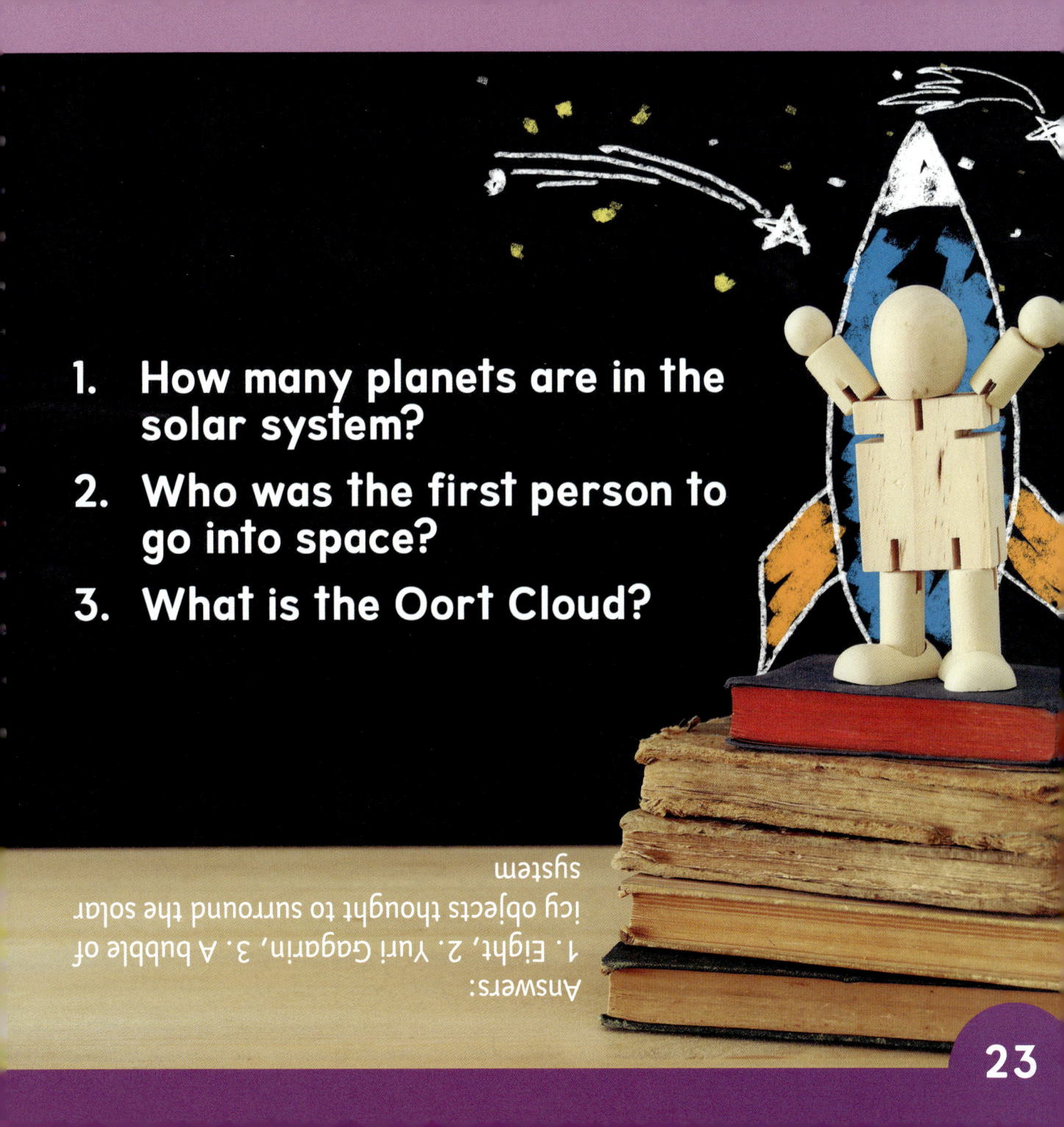

Answers:
1. Eight, 2. Yuri Gagarin, 3. A bubble of icy objects thought to surround the solar system

23

GLOSSARY

atmosphere   the mixture of gases that makes up the air and surrounds Earth

force   a push or pull on an object

launched   sent off, such as into space or out onto water

mnemonic device   a memory tool, such as a phrase or song, to help someone remember something

orbital path   the repeated path one object takes around another object

universe   everything that exists

INDEX